Cover design by Bill Johnson

Library of Congress Cataloging-in-Publication Data:

Eckhardt, John, 1957-
  Prayers that release heaven on earth / John Eckhardt. -- 1st ed.
      p. cm.
  Includes bibliographical references.
  ISBN 978-1-61638-003-8
  1.   Kingdom of God--Biblical teaching. 2.   Kingdom of God--Prayers and devotions. I. Title.

  BS680.K52E34 2010
  236'.9--dc22

                                                2010014315

E-book ISBN: 978-1-61638-266-7

Available in Spanish as *Oraciones que revelan el cielo en la tierra*, copyright © 2010 by John Eckhardt, published by Casa Creación, a Strang company. All rights reserved.

10 11 12 13 14 — 9 8 7 6 5 4 3 2
Printed in the United States of America

HAIL TO THE LORD'S ANOINTED

1. Hail to the Lord's Anointed,
Great David's greater Son!
Hail, in the time appointed,
His reign on Earth begun!
He comes to break oppression,
To set the captive free,
To take away transgression,
And rule in equity.

2. He comes with succor speedy
To those who suffer wrong;
To help the poor and needy,
And bid the weak be strong;
To give them songs for sighing;
Their darkness turn to light,
Whose souls, condemned and dying,
Were precious in His sight.

3. He shall come down like showers
Upon the fruitful earth;
And love, joy, hope, like flowers,
Spring in His path to birth.
Before Him on the mountains

Shall peace, the herald, go;
And righteousness, in fountains,
From hill to valley flow.

4. Arabia's desert ranger
To Him shall bow the knee;
The Ethiopian stranger
His glory come to see;
With offerings of devotion
Ships from the isles shall meet,
To pour the wealth of ocean
In tribute at His feet.

5. For Him shall prayer unceasing
And daily vows ascend;
His kingdom still increasing,
A kingdom without end.
The tide of time shall never
His covenant remove;
His name shall stand forever;
That name to us is Love.

6. The heav'ns which now conceal Him,
In counsels deep and wise,
In glory shall reveal Him
To our rejoicing eyes;
He who, with hands uplifted,

When from the earth below,
Shall come again all gifted,
His blessings to bestow.

7. Kings shall fall down before Him,
And gold and incense bring,
All nations shall adore Him,
His praise the people sing.
Outstretched His wide dominion,
O'er river, sea and shore,
Far as eagle's pinion,
Or dove's light wing can soar.

8. O'er every foe victorious,
He on His throne shall rest;
From age to age more glorious,
All-blessing and all-blest.
The tide of time shall never
His covenant remove;
His name shall stand for ever,
His changeless name of Love.*

—James Montgomery

---

* "Hail to the Lord's Anointed," words by James Montgomery, a
paraphrase of Psalm 72, written December 1821, published 1822.
Public domain.

CONTENTS

"Hail to the Lord's Anointed" iv

Introduction..1

Section 1
Understanding God's Plan

1   God's Plan for a Kingdom.......................................7

2   God's Plan Will Release Heaven on Earth........ 11

3   God's Plan Is Revealed Through the Gospel.....21

4   God's Plan for the Gentiles...................................27

Section 2
Prayers and Decrees for God's Plan
to be Fulfilled... 39

INTRODUCTION

G OD HAS A marvelous plan for His church, a plan that will help release heaven on the earth. The prophets predicted a time when salvation, righteousness, peace, joy, rejoicing, and redemption will come to Israel and the world. Jerusalem (Zion) will be restored and once again become the dwelling place of God. The heathen (nations) will come to the God of Israel and worship. It will be a time of the establishing of an everlasting covenant (new covenant). God's plans are for a time when old things (former things) pass away and new things spring forth. There will be an outpouring of the Holy Spirit and the release of living waters from Jerusalem, which will flow to the nations.

It is time for God's people to get on board with God's plan and to diligently pray—and work—to see the fulfillment of God's plan for His church.

1

God has given us a clear mandate for what we should be doing. He says:

> If My people who are called by My name will humble themselves, and pray and seek My face, and turn from their wicked ways, then I will hear from heaven, and will forgive their sin and heal their land.
>
> —2 Chronicles 7:14

I have written this book for you to understand thoroughly that God's plan is to establish and advance His kingdom. As you read, may your heart be stirred with a longing for the fulfillment of God's plan to release heaven on the earth. Be filled with hope for an earth filled with His righteousness. See how God's plan is unveiled in the pages of the Gospels. Get excited to challenge yourself to diligently pray for God's plan—God's kingdom, heaven—to be released on Earth *now*.

In Section II of this book you will find hundreds of prayers and decrees that will help you to keep your mind and heart focused on the plan of God.

Use the words of Isaiah as your call to others: "Of the increase of His government and peace there will be no end, upon the throne of David and over His kingdom, to order it and establish it with judgment and justice from that time forward, even forever. The zeal of the LORD of hosts will perform this" (Isa. 9:7).

SECTION 1

UNDERSTANDING GOD'S PLAN

CHAPTER 1

GOD'S PLAN FOR A KINGDOM

T HE ESTABLISHMENT OF the kingdom of God included the restoration of the tabernacle of David (Acts 15) with the coming of the Gentiles into the church. The righteous will flourish, and the earth will be filled with the knowledge of the Lord. God plans to accomplish all of this through the Messiah-King, His Son, Jesus Christ.

During Bible times, the prophets saw the coming kingdom as a time of great joy and rejoicing. They prophesied that everlasting joy would be upon the head of the righteous, and they would obtain gladness and joy (Isa. 35:10; 51:11). Zion would be the joy of many generations (Isa. 60:15). Those who believe the gospel would receive the oil of joy

(Isa. 61:1–3), and they would receive everlasting joy (v. 7).

The Lord would cause rejoicing to fill Jerusalem and to fill her people with joy (Isa. 65:19). This indicates new-covenant Jerusalem, the church (Heb. 12:22). The nations would be glad and sing for joy because of the rule of Messiah (Ps. 67:4). Mount Zion (the church) rejoices (Ps. 48:11).

Israel had never experienced earthly peace for any extended period of time. The peace they desire would come only through Messiah, and it would be spiritual. The peace they needed was hidden from their eyes, and it was prophesied that they would experience a Roman invasion (Luke 19:41–44). They were looking for an earthly peace and missed the spiritual peace that comes through Christ. *Peace* is the Hebrew word *shalom*, meaning "prosperity, health, wholeness."

Jesus is the Prince of Peace (Isa. 9:6). The increase of His government and peace will have no end (v. 7). The gospel is called the *gospel of peace* (Rom. 10:15). Fulfillment of the kingdom of God began to come to the nations because of the preaching of the gospel. Today the preaching of the gospel is still taking place, and as believers we can usher in God's kingdom plan through our prayers. Those who preach the gospel publish peace, which is part of the plan of God for His kingdom (Isa. 52:7; Nah. 1:15). The new covenant is the covenant of peace (Isa. 54:10; Ezek. 34:25; 37:26), and the prayers of believers fulfill the plan of God and expand the peace of God.

The prophets spoke of the coming kingdom in terms of peace. The King would bring peace to the people (Ps. 72:3), and the righteous would have an abundance of peace (v. 7). The Lord would ordain peace for His people (Isa. 26:12). The work of righteousness would be peace (Isa. 32:17). The kingdom of peace would come through the suffering of the Messiah. The chastisement of our peace was upon Him (Isa. 53:5). We are led forth with peace (Isa. 55:12). God would extend peace like a river (Isa. 66:12). He would speak peace to the heathen (Zech. 9:10).

It is God's plan that righteousness would reign in His kingdom. The Old Testament is filled with references to the righteousness of the kingdom. In the New Testament, we learn that we are made the righteousness of God in Christ (2 Cor. 5:21). He is our righteousness (1 Cor. 1:30). Israel could not attain righteousness through the Law. Righteousness comes through faith and the new covenant. Today, as believers in Christ and His righteousness, we are living in the kingdom. The Christian—the new man—is created in righteousness and true holiness (Eph. 4:24). Yet we have not yet experienced a world filled with peace and righteousness. As we pray these prayers, we can expect righteousness, peace, and joy to increase from generation to generation.

CHAPTER 2

GOD'S PLAN WILL RELEASE HEAVEN ON EARTH

THE ANNOUNCEMENT OF the nearness of the kingdom was an announcement of the coming righteousness of the kingdom. This righteousness would come through the gospel (Rom. 1:17). The righteousness of the kingdom could not come by the Law, but through faith in the Messiah. God's plan will not take place through worldly things (meat and drink). His plan is for a spiritual kingdom, one that is filled with His righteousness.

The Jews were looking for an earthly kingdom and missed the righteousness that comes by faith. Many missed the kingdom and the righteousness that comes through faith in the gospel. Today, many people—including Christians—are still not

11

seeing God's plan fulfilled because they are looking at earthly solutions for God's spiritual kingdom. We must strengthen our faith in God's power to usher in His kingdom and pray diligently for His plan to be unfolded.

The prophets spoke of the coming righteousness of the kingdom. The kingdom is connected to the gospel (Isa. 52:7). The righteousness of God would come to Israel and the nations through the gospel. Many in Israel missed the kingdom because they did not obey the gospel (Rom. 10:15–16). They did not submit to the gospel. They did not submit to the righteousness of God (v. 3). They became enemies of the gospel and therefore enemies of the kingdom (Rom. 11:28; 1 Thess. 2:14–16).

Today we must pray earnestly for righteousness to come to our homes, our communities, our nation, and our world. We must pray that the world's rampant disobedience to the plans and will of God will cease. We must pray for people to turn in obedience to God! Pray that the righteousness of

God will come to the nations of the world and to the homes of people throughout our world.

We learn in Isaiah 32:17 that the work of righteousness will be demonstrated in peace (*shalom*), and that the work of righteousness will demonstrate quietness and confidence. As we pray in quietness and confidence for this to happen today, our prayers will include these characteristics of God's plan:

- Righteousness will be revealed (Isa. 56:1).
- The saints will be called trees of righteousness (Isa. 61:3).
- Righteousness and praise will spring forth among the nations (Isa. 61:11).
- The Messiah will bring in everlasting righteousness (Dan. 9:24).
- The new man—new believers—will be created in righteousness (Eph. 4:24).
- The new covenant will administrate righteousness (2 Cor. 3:9).
- The scepter of the kingdom will be righteousness (Heb. 1:8).

- The righteous will flourish in the days of the Messiah (the kingdom—Ps. 72:7).

How marvelous it will be when the plans of God for His kingdom can permeate every corner of this world. The Bible tells us that "the righteous will be planted in the land" (Isa. 60:21). Can you imagine the time when America has so many righteous believers "planted" throughout its regions that our entire nation is known in today's world as a righteous land?

Unfortunately, today America is recognized throughout the world as a nation that is straying away from its righteous foundations. Instead of righteousness filling our streets, we have rebellion against God, and wickedness and sin that are terrifying the people of America. If the people of America—and of the nations—are to be recognized as the planting of the Lord, we must pray for God to have mercy on our rebelliousness and sinfulness and to call us to repentance. America must turn back to the godly foundations upon which it was birthed. As you read these pages, commit to praying diligently for the plans of God to be fulfilled in America and throughout the world so that the plan of God and the kingdom of God can be established.

We will become the planting of the Lord only as we place our faith and trust in the gospel (Isa. 61:1–3). An earthly kingdom requires an earthly land, but a spiritual kingdom does not. We must recognize that we are praying for a spiritual kingdom. The Bible tells us that Abraham was not looking for an earthly land but a heavenly country (Heb. 11:14–16). We must be seeking a heavenly America today.

It is God's plan to fill the world with righteousness. The Old Testament is filled with references to the righteousness of the kingdom. We are made the righteousness of God in Christ (2 Cor. 5:21). Christ is our righteousness (1 Cor. 1:30). Israel could not attain righteousness through the Law. Righteousness comes through faith and the new covenant. We are now living in the kingdom and the new covenant.

As you pray, thank God that He has fulfilled His plan through Christ, His Son. Include the following promises in your prayers.

PRAYERS

Lord, we pray that "all the mighty ones upon earth…shall come and shall declare His righteousness to a people yet to be born—that He has done it [that it is finished]!" (Ps. 22:29, 31, AMP).

Lord, may I be able to say, "I have proclaimed glad tidings of righteousness in the great congregation; behold, I will not restrain my lips, O LORD, You know. I have not hidden Your righteousness within my heart; I have spoken of Your faithfulness and Your salvation; I have not concealed Your lovingkindness and Your truth from the great congregation" (Ps. 40:9–10, NAS).

Lord, "let the heavens declare His righteousness, for God Himself is Judge" (Ps. 50:6).

Lord, "my adversaries are all before You [fully known to You]....Let one [unforgiven] perverseness and iniquity accumulate upon another for them [in Your book], and let them not come into Your righteousness or be justified and acquitted by You. Let them be blotted out of the book of the living and the book of life and not be enrolled among the [uncompromisingly] righteous (those upright and in right standing with God)" (Ps. 69:19, 27–28, AMP).

Father, "my mouth shall tell of Your righteousness and Your salvation all the day, for I do not know their limits. I will go in the strength of the Lord GOD; I will make mention of Your righteousness, of Yours only" (Ps. 71:15–16).

"Your righteousness reaches to the skies, O God, you who have done great things. Who, O God, is like you?" (Ps. 71:19, NIV).

Father, I pray that the prayer of Solomon will be true in the nations today: "Give the gift of wise rule to the king, O God, the gift of just rule to the crown prince. May he judge your people rightly, be honorable to your meek and lowly....Please stand up for the poor, help the children of the needy, come down hard on the cruel tyrants....Let righteousness burst into blossom and peace abound until the moon fades to nothing. Rule from sea to sea" (Ps. 72:1–8, THE MESSAGE).

Lord, my prayer will continually rise to You until our nation reflects Your Word, which promises: "Love and faithfulness meet together; righteousness and peace kiss each other. Faithfulness springs forth from the earth, and righteousness looks down from heaven....Righteousness goes before him and prepares the way for his steps" (Ps. 85:10–11, 13, NIV).

Father, "blessed are those who have learned to acclaim you, who walk in the light of your presence, O LORD. They rejoice in your name all day long; they exult in your righteousness. For you are their glory and strength" (Ps. 89:15–17, NIV).

Father, hear our prayers for the nations, that "the LORD will not reject his people; he will never forsake his inheritance. Judgment will again be founded on righteousness, and all the upright in heart will follow it" (Ps. 94:14–15, NIV).

"The LORD reigns, let the earth be glad; let the distant shores rejoice.... The heavens proclaim his righteousness, and all the peoples see his glory" (Ps. 97:1, 6, NIV).

Lord, I praise You because Your Word has promised: "The LORD has made his salvation known and revealed his righteousness to the nations. He has remembered his love and his faithfulness to the house of Israel; all the ends of the earth have seen the salvation of our God" (Ps. 98:2–3, NIV).

Father, I praise You because "from everlasting to everlasting the LORD's love is with those who fear him, and his righteousness with their children's children" (Ps. 103:17, NIV).

Lord, with the psalmist, I will declare, "Praise the LORD. I will extol the LORD with all my heart in the council of the upright and in the assembly. Great are the works of the LORD; they are pondered by all who delight in them. Glorious and majestic are his deeds, and his righteousness endures forever" (Ps. 111:1–3, NIV).

Father, this is the prayer of my heart: "Open for me the gates of righteousness; I will enter and give thanks to the LORD. This is the gate of the LORD through which the righteous may enter. I will give you thanks, for you answered me; you have become my salvation" (Ps. 118:19–21, NIV).

CHAPTER 3

GOD'S PLAN IS REVEALED THROUGH THE GOSPEL

THE KINGDOM IS a mystery. The joining of Jew and Gentile in the church is a mystery (Eph. 3:1–6). It has been given unto us to know the mysteries of the kingdom (Mark 4:11). The plan of God was to establish His kingdom through the church; when this is done, heaven will be released on the earth. The church made known to the principalities and powers the manifold wisdom of God (Eph. 3:10). The kingdom was the eternal purpose of God in Christ (v. 11).

Jesus Christ (the Anointed One) is the key to the fulfillment of these kingdom promises. Jesus was anointed to bring the message of the kingdom and to establish the kingdom. We are now living in the days of the Messiah-King. We can enjoy the blessings of the kingdom and pray for the kingdom to advance. Of the increase of His government (kingdom) and peace (*shalom*) there will be no end. The kingdom is from generation to generation. Our prayers and decrees help advance the kingdom in our generation and prepare the way for generations to come.

The kingdom of God is connected to the gospel. To preach the gospel is to preach the kingdom. When Jesus walked on earth, He proclaimed: "The time is fulfilled, and the kingdom of God is at hand. Repent, and believe in the gospel" (Mark 1:15).

The gospel is a declaration of the reign of God.

> How beautiful upon the mountains
> Are the feet of him who brings good news,
> Who proclaims peace,
> Who brings glad tidings of good things,
> Who proclaims salvation,
> Who says to Zion,
> "Your God reigns!"
>
> —Isaiah 52:7

God's Plan Is Revealed Through the Gospel

It is God's plan to reign over the heathen through the preaching of the gospel. "God reigns over the nations; God sits on His holy throne" (Ps. 47:8). The reign of God is a heavenly, spiritual reign over the nations. It is not a physical or geographical reign. There is no substitute for the preaching of the gospel.

The gospel of the kingdom is the gospel of peace. The enemies of the gospel are the enemies of the kingdom. They are also the enemies of peace. But God has proclaimed, "How beautiful are the feet of those who bring glad tidings! [How welcome is the coming of those who preach the good news of His good things!]" (Rom. 10:15, AMP).

The gospel of the kingdom is also the gospel of Christ. To preach Christ is to preach the kingdom. To submit to Christ is to submit to the kingdom. The gospel was preached to Abraham. Through his seed would all the families of the earth be blessed. This is fulfilled through Christ and the gospel. And today, the plan of God is that the nations will be justified through faith in Jesus Christ.

> The Scripture foresaw that God would justify the Gentiles by faith, and announced the gospel in advance to Abraham: "All nations will be blessed through you."
>
> —Galatians 3:8, NIV

The kingdom is a mystery, and so is the gospel. When we pray for the mysteries of God to be revealed, we are praying for the mystery of the kingdom to be revealed. The apostle Paul prayed:

> Pray also for me, that whenever I open my mouth, words may be given me so that I will fearlessly make known the mystery of the gospel.
>
> —Ephesians 6:19, NIV

God's plan—God's kingdom, the release of heaven on earth—is revealed through the gospel:

> Now to him who is able to establish you by my gospel and the proclamation of Jesus Christ, according to the revelation of the mystery hidden for long ages past, but

now revealed and made known through the prophetic writings by the command of the eternal God, so that all nations might believe and obey him.

—Romans 16:25–26, NIV

We pray that the word of the Lord would have free course. This is praying for the kingdom to advance.

Finally, brothers, pray for us that the message of the Lord may spread rapidly and be honored, just as it was with you.

—2 Thessalonians 3:1, NIV

CHAPTER 4

GOD'S PLAN FOR THE GENTILES

IT IS THE plan of God that the kingdom of God have dominion over the Gentiles. "He shall have dominion also from sea to sea, and from the River to the ends of the earth" (Ps. 72:8).

Israel had the promise of the nations being subdued under them. "For the LORD Most High is awesome; He is a great King over all the earth. He will subdue the peoples under us, and the nations under our feet" (Ps. 47:2–3).

This plan would come to pass through Messiah. Many in Israel viewed this promise as a physical dominion over the Gentiles. The rule over the Gentiles through Christ was being fulfilled in the first century (Rom. 15:8–12). It is fulfilled through

PRAYERS THAT RELEASE HEAVEN ON EARTH

Christ and the church. The Gentiles were coming into the tabernacle of David (Acts 15:15–17). The tabernacle of David was the rule of Christ, the son of David. There is, however, no physical dominion of Israel over the Gentiles. The kingdom is not physical, but spiritual.

The nations were being subdued through the gospel. The gospel was to the Jew first. The nations were being saved through the Jewish Messiah. The dominion was spiritual. The nations were coming under the reign of Christ in fulfillment of Isaiah 11:10. Israel's glory would be the salvation of the Gentiles (Isa. 60).

Many in Israel missed this glory because they were expecting a worldly kingdom instead of a heavenly kingdom. Instead of rejoicing in the salvation of the nations, many in Israel opposed the gospel. The nations were being subdued to Israel through their Messiah, yet many missed it because they were looking for a kingdom with observation (Luke 17:20–21). The Gentiles were submitting to the kingdom through the gospel.

Israel never subdued their enemies for any extended period of time. They usually were under Gentile dominion. Military conquest would not be the fulfillment of dominion promises. Christ would subdue the nations through the gospel of peace. The kingdom is not advanced through the sword but through preaching.

Christ did subdue the enemies of the kingdom, and there are references to warfare in the Book of Revelation. The enemies of the kingdom were the first-century generation that opposed the gospel and persecuted the church. Christ subdued the nations through the gospel, and He subdued His enemies through judgment.

The following old covenant promises are fulfilled in Christ:

> All the ends of the world
> Shall remember and turn to the LORD,
> And all the families of the nations
> Shall worship before You.
> For the kingdom is the LORD's,

And He rules over the nations.

—Psalm 22:27–28

I will praise You, O Lord, among the
peoples;
I will sing to You among the nations.

—Psalm 57:9

That Your way may be known on earth,
Your salvation among all nations.

—Psalm 67:2

Oh, let the nations be glad and sing for
joy!

—Psalm 67:4

Yes, all kings shall fall down before Him;
All nations shall serve Him.

—Psalm 72:11

All nations shall call Him blessed.

—Psalm 72:17

Arise, O God, judge the earth;
For You shall inherit all nations.

—Psalm 82:8

All nations whom You have made
Shall come and worship before You, O
   Lord,
And shall glorify Your name.

—Psalm 86:9

I will praise You, O LORD, among the
   peoples,
And I will sing praises to You among the
   nations.

—Psalm 108:3

Praise the LORD, all you Gentiles!
Laud Him, all you peoples!

—Psalm 117:1

These scriptures could never be completely fulfilled under the old covenant. The heathen (nations) were in darkness. They were "aliens from the commonwealth of Israel and strangers from the covenants of promise, having no hope and without God in the world" (Eph. 2:12). These scriptures can be fulfilled only in Christ, through the church, under the new covenant, in the present kingdom age.

Praise and worship among the nations are the manifestation of the kingdom. The Gentiles would glorify God for His mercy.

> And that the Gentiles might glorify God for His mercy, as it is written:
>
> "For this reason I will confess to You among the Gentiles,
> And sing to Your name."
>
> And again he says:
>
> "Rejoice, O Gentiles, with His people!"
>
> And again:
>
> "Praise the LORD, all you Gentiles!
> Laud Him, all you peoples!"
>
> And again, Isaiah says:
>
> "There shall be a root of Jesse;
> And He who shall rise to reign over the Gentiles,

In Him the Gentiles shall hope."
—Romans 15:9–12

Paul quotes Psalm 117 and Isaiah 11 as being fulfilled in Christ and the church. God's mercy on Israel, through Christ, resulted in salvation coming to the Gentiles (nations). The gospel came to the Jew first. Many Jews responded and were saved. The Gentiles responded to the gospel, and both were made one in Christ. Worship is no longer connected to earthly Jerusalem, but is done in Spirit and truth (John 4:21–24).

> The Spirit of the Lord GOD is upon me; because the LORD hath anointed me to preach good tidings unto the meek; he hath sent me to bind up the brokenhearted, to proclaim liberty to the captives, and the opening of the prison to them that are bound; to proclaim the acceptable year of the LORD, and the day of vengeance of our God; to comfort all that mourn; to appoint unto them that mourn in Zion, to give

unto them beauty for ashes, the oil of joy for mourning, the garment of praise for the spirit of heaviness; that they might be called trees of righteousness, the planting of the LORD, that he might be glorified.

—Isaiah 61:1–3, KJV

Behold my servant, whom I uphold; mine elect, in whom my soul delighteth; I have put my spirit upon him: he shall bring forth judgment to the Gentiles. He shall not cry, nor lift up, nor cause his voice to be heard in the street. A bruised reed shall he not break, and the smoking flax shall he not quench: he shall bring forth judgment unto truth. He shall not fail nor be discouraged, till he have set judgment in the earth: and the isles shall wait for his law.

—Isaiah 42:1–4, KJV

The kingdom does not come with observation (Luke 17:20). Many in Israel were looking for an earthly kingdom. They were disappointed, and many rejected Christ because He was not an earthly king. Jesus said His kingdom was not of this world. The kingdom is not meat and drink, but righteousness, peace, and joy in the Holy Ghost (Rom. 14:17). The kingdom is spiritual and heavenly.

Jesus told Nicodemus that he must be born again to see the kingdom (John 3:3). In other words, entrance into the kingdom is not by physical birth or genealogy. Physical descent from Abraham did not qualify one to enter the kingdom. The kingdom is spiritual and can be entered into only by spiritual birth.

The language of the prophets is poetic and figurative. The heavens, earth, seas, trees, and waves are commanded to praise the Lord. These are figurative words used to describe nations and peoples. God uses natural symbols and figures to describe spiritual realities. The old covenant types and symbols are present-day realities for the new covenant believer. Righteousness, peace, and joy of the kingdom are found in Christ and His church.

The kingdom of God is within us (Luke 17:21).

The kingdom is Christ in us. You cannot separate Christ and His kingdom. Ezekiel saw a river flowing from the temple, and out of our bellies flow rivers of living water. The kingdom is like a river; it flows from Zion to the nations. Wherever the river goes, it brings healing (Ezek. 47).

One problem we have in understanding "the kingdom of God" is that we think of a kingdom as being a piece of land with fixed boundaries. We think of a place. But in ancient days a king's *kingdom* extended to wherever he could exercise his power. There were no fixed boundaries. Boundaries were fluid and continually changing. The people, therefore, thought in terms of kingly rule. The *kingdom* was the sphere over which each ruler ruled, regardless of boundaries. It was similar to the Bedouin chieftain who is *king* over his people as they travel around in the deserts, no matter where they are. Wherever he is, and wherever he exercises his power, regardless of location, he is king. Thus if his men surround you in the desert because you chance to be where they are, you are in his *kingdom*; you are under his kingly rule. And next year, or even month, the same spot may be under the kingly rule of a Bedouin chieftain of another tribe, while your king is a hundred miles away having taken his *kingdom* with him. They rule over the people, not the land. The word *basileia*, therefore, means, "kingly rule" rather than "kingdom," and it points to submission to a king.*

God's kingdom is evident when the nations come to Zion and worship. We have not come to earthly Zion but to heavenly Zion. The books of the prophets are filled with references to the nations (heathen) coming to worship. This is not a geographical or political nation, but people groups being saved and coming to worship. This has been happening for the past two millennia, and it is happening today.

> But you have come to Mount Zion and to the city of the living God, the heavenly

---

* Angelfire.com, "The Kingdom of God in the New Testament," http://www.angelfire.com/planet/lifetruth/kingdomnew.html (accessed March 26, 2010).

Jerusalem, to an innumerable company of angels.

—Hebrews 12:22

We have come to Zion, and we are praying that others will come now and in generations to come. The kingdom is not geographical (physical), but it is evident wherever men submit their hearts to the rule of the king. And as this is done, heaven will be released on Earth.

SECTION 2

PRAYERS AND DECREES
TO RELEASE HEAVEN
ON EARTH

Lord, Your scepter of leadership comes from Judah, and when You come and reveal Yourself as the Messiah, the nations will gather to You in obedience (Gen. 49:10, AMP).

Lord, Your kingdom is higher than Agag (the kingdom of the Gentiles), and Your kingdom is exalted above all others (Num. 24:7, AMP).

Lord, You are the Star out of Jacob, and You smote the corners of Moab (symbolic enemies of Christ and His church) and destroyed the children of Seth (Moab's sons of tumult) (Num. 24:17, AMP).

Lord, You have been set upon the holy hill of Zion, and You will rule in the midst of Your enemies (Ps. 2:6; 110:2).

Lord, the nations are Your inheritance, and the uttermost parts of the earth Your possession (Ps. 2:8).

Break the nations with Your rod of iron (Ps. 2:9)

Let the kings and judges of the earth be wise, and serve the Lord with reverent awe and worshipful fear, and rejoice with trembling (Ps. 2:10–11).

I will lay me down and sleep, for You, Lord, have sustained me (Ps. 3:5).

Lord, Your blessing is upon my life (Ps. 3:8).

Let the nations offer the sacrifices of righteousness and put their trust in the Lord (Ps. 4:5).

I will lie down and sleep in peace, for You alone, O Lord, make me dwell in safety (Ps. 4:8).

Give heed to the voice of my cry, my King and my God, for to You I will pray (Ps. 5:2).

My voice You shall hear in the morning, O Lord; in the morning I will direct it to You, and I will look up (Ps. 5:3).

Because of your great mercy, I come to Your house, Lord, and I am filled with wonder as I bow down to worship at Your holy temple (Ps. 5:7, CEV).

Lead me, O Lord, in Your righteousness because of my enemies; make Your way straight before my face (Ps. 5:8).

Lord, You have blessed me, and You surround my life with favor (Ps. 5:12).

The Lord has heard my supplication; the Lord will receive my prayer (Ps. 6:9).

My defense is of God, who saves the upright in heart (Ps. 7:10).

Lord, You let us rule everything Your hands have made. And You put all of it under our power—the sheep and the cattle, and every wild animal, the birds in the sky, the fish in the sea, and all ocean creatures. Our Lord and Ruler, Your name is wonderful everywhere on earth! (Ps. 8:6–9, CEV).

Lord, You shall endure forever, and You have prepared Your throne for judgment (Ps. 9:7).

I dwell in Zion, and I will sing praises unto the Lord and declare Your doings among the people (Ps. 9:11).

Once you've pulled me back from the gates of death, I'll write the book on Hallelujahs; on the corner of Main and First I'll hold a street meeting; I'll be the song leader; we'll fill the air with salvation songs (Ps. 9:13–14, THE MESSAGE).

Put them in fear, O Lord, that the nations may know themselves to be but men (Ps. 9:20).

Arise, O Lord! O God, lift up Your hand! Do not forget the humble (Ps. 10:12).

Our Lord, You will always rule, but nations will vanish from the earth (Ps. 10:16, CEV).

You have been good to me, Lord, and I will sing about You (Ps. 13:6, CEV).

Lord, Your salvation has come out of Zion, and You have brought back the captivity of Your people; I will rejoice and be glad (Ps. 14:7).

I abide in Your tabernacle, and I dwell in Your holy hill, and I will never be moved (Ps. 15:1, 5).

You, Lord, are all I want! You are my choice, and You keep me safe. You make my life pleasant, and my future is bright (Ps. 16:5–6, CEV).

You have made known to me the path of life; You will fill me with joy in Your presence, with eternal pleasures at Your right hand (Ps. 16:11, NIV).

Lord, may my steps always hold closely to Your paths [to the tracks of the One Who has gone on before]; then my feet will not slip from Your paths (Ps. 17:5, AMP).

Keep and guard me as the pupil of Your eye; hide me in the shadow of Your wings (Ps. 17:8, AMP).

Lord, You have promised to light my lamp and to enlighten my darkness (Ps. 18:28).

Lord, because of Your power in me, I can advance against my enemies and scale the walls intended to keep me out (Ps. 18:29, NIV).

Lord, it is You who arms me with strength and makes my way perfect (Ps. 18:32, NIV).

Lord, You give me your shield of victory, and Your right hand sustains me; You stoop down to make me great (Ps. 18:35).

Lord, You enlarge the path under me, so that my feet will not slip (Ps. 18:36).

Let strangers submit to You when they hear of You (Ps. 18:44).

Lord, the heavens declare Your glory, and the skies proclaim the work of Your hands. Your voice has gone out into all the earth, and Your words to the ends of the world (Ps. 19:1, NIV; Rom. 10:18, NIV).

Save, Lord. You are the King; hear me when I call (Ps. 20:9).

Show your strength, Lord, so that we may sing and praise Your power (Ps. 21:13, CEV).

Lord, You inhabit my praise; You are holy (Ps. 22:3).

Lord, everyone on this earth will remember You. People all over the world will turn and worship You, because You are in control, the ruler of all nations (Ps. 22:27–28, CEV).

Surely goodness and mercy shall follow me all the days of my life, and I will dwell in the house of the Lord forever (Ps. 23:6).

Lord, the everlasting gates have opened for You, and You are the King of glory (Ps. 24:7–10).

Show me Your ways, O Lord; teach me Your paths. Lead me in Your truth and teach me, for You are the God of my salvation; on You I wait all the day (Ps. 25:4–5).

Lord, You guide the humble in justice, and You teach the humble Your way (Ps. 25:9).

Lord, because I fear You, You will reveal Your secret to me and will show me Your covenant (Ps. 25:14).

Lord, You are my light and my salvation; whom shall I fear? You are the strength of my life; of whom shall I be afraid? (Ps. 27:1).

One thing I have desired of the Lord, that will I seek: That I may dwell in the house of the Lord all the days of my life, to behold the beauty of the Lord and to inquire in His temple (Ps. 27:4).

Lord, You are my strength and my shield; my heart trusts in You, and I am helped; therefore my heart greatly rejoices, and with my song I will praise You (Ps. 28:7).

Lord, Your voice is powerful, and Your voice is full of majesty (Ps. 29:4).

Lord, the thunder of Your voice can break the cedars into pieces (Ps. 29:5).

Your voice splits and flashes forth forked lightning (Ps. 29:7, AMP).

Lord, Your voice makes the wilderness tremble (Ps. 29:8, AMP).

The voice of the Lord makes deer give birth before their time (Ps. 29:9, CEV).

You have turned for me my mourning into dancing; You have put off my sackcloth and clothed me with gladness (Ps. 30:11).

Blessed be the Lord, for He has shown me His marvelous kindness in a strong city [Zion]! (Ps. 31:21).

My transgression is forgiven, and my sin is covered. I am blessed, my sin is not imputed to me, and there is no guile in my life (Ps. 32:1–2).

Lord, surround me with songs of deliverance (Ps. 32:7).

Let all the earth fear the Lord; let all the inhabitants of the world stand in awe of Him (Ps. 33:8).

Blessed is the nation whose God is the Lord, and the people He has chosen as His own inheritance. I am blessed, and I am a part of the holy nation [the church] (Ps. 33:12; 1 Pet. 2:9).

I put my trust under the shadow of Your wings. I will be abundantly satisfied with the fullness of Your house, and You will give me drink from the river of Your pleasures. With You is the fountain of life, and in Your light I will see light (Ps. 36:7–9).

I delight myself in the Lord, and He gives me the desires of my heart (Ps. 37:4).

I inherit the land, and I delight myself in the abundance of peace [shalom] (Ps. 37:11).

Let me not be ashamed in the evil time, and let me be satisfied in the days of famine (Ps. 37:19).

I will wait on You, Lord, and keep Your way; let me be exalted to inherit the land (Ps. 37:34).

Lord, put a new song in my mouth, even praise to You, that many will see it and fear and will trust in the Lord (Ps. 40:3).

I will go with Your people to the house of God with the voice of joy and praise; I will join with them that keep Your festival (Ps. 42:4).

O send out Your light and Your truth. Let them bring me to Your holy hill and to Your dwelling places (Ps. 43:3).

I will worship at Your altar because You make me joyful. You are my God, and I will praise You. Yes, I will praise You as I play my harp (Ps. 43:4, CEV).

Your throne, O God, is forever and ever; a scepter of righteousness is the scepter of Your kingdom. Let the scepter of Your kingdom be stretched over the nations (Ps. 45:6).

There is a river whose streams make glad the city of God, the holy place where the Most High dwells (Ps. 46:4, NIV).

Let the nations be still and know that You are God; be exalted among the nations, and be exalted in the earth (Ps. 46:10).

For the Lord Most High is awesome; He is the great King over all the earth. He will subdue the peoples under us, and the nations under our feet (Ps. 47:2–3).

Let me receive the inheritance You have chosen for me, the glory and pride of Jacob, whom You loved (Ps. 47:4, AMP).

I will sing praises to You, O Lord, my king. You are king over all the earth (Ps. 47:7).

Lord, You reign over the nations; You sit upon the throne of Your holiness (Ps. 47:8).

Let the nobles of the nations assemble as the people of the God of Abraham, for the kings of the earth belong to You (Ps. 47:9).

Lord, You are greatly to be praised in Zion [the church], the city of God, the mountain of Your holiness (Ps. 48:1).

Let Zion be established forever (Ps. 48:8).

Let Mount Zion rejoice, let the daughters of Judah be glad, because of Your judgments (Ps. 48:11).

Lord, let the people, all the inhabitants of the world, give ear and hear Your wisdom. Let them hear and understand Your parables of the kingdom (Ps. 49:1–4).

Lord, speak, and call the earth from the rising of the sun to its going down; out of Zion, let the perfection of Your beauty shine forth (Ps. 50:1–2).

O Lord, open my lips, and my mouth shall show forth Your praise (Ps. 51:15).

Make Zion [the church] the place you delight in; repair Jerusalem's broken-down walls (Ps. 51:18, THE MESSAGE).

But I am like a green olive tree in the house of God; I will trust in the mercy of God forever and ever (Ps. 52:8).

O Lord, Your salvation has come out of Zion, and You have brought back the captivity of Your people; I will rejoice and be glad (Ps. 53:6).

I will freely sacrifice to You; I will praise Your name, O Lord, for it is good (Ps. 54:6).

I cast my burden upon You, Lord, and You will sustain me; You will never permit me to be moved (Ps. 55:22).

In God, whose word I praise, in the Lord, whose word I praise—in God I trust; I will not be afraid. What can man do to me? (Ps. 56:10–11, NIV).

I will praise You, O Lord, among the peoples; I will sing to You among the nations. For Your mercy reaches unto the heavens, and Your truth unto the clouds (Ps. 57:9–10).

Be exalted, O God, above the heavens; let Your glory be above all the earth (Ps. 57:11).

I will sing of Your power, and I will sing aloud of Your mercy, for You have been my defense and refuge in the day of trouble (Ps. 59:16).

Lord, give me Your banner, and let it be displayed because of truth (Ps. 60:4).

Through God I will do valiantly, for it is He who shall tread down our enemies (Ps. 60:12).

I will abide in Your tabernacle forever; I will trust in the shelter of Your wings (Ps. 61:4).

Lord, release Your power, for power belongs to You (Ps. 62:11).

Lord, I have seen you in the sanctuary; let me behold Your power and Your glory (Ps. 63:2).

Lord, my soul will be satisfied as with the richest of foods; with singing lips my mouth will praise You (Ps. 63:5).

Hide me from the secret plots of the wicked, from the rebellion of the workers of iniquity (Ps. 64:2).

Let all flesh come unto You, because You hear prayer (Ps. 65:2).

Bring Your chosen ones near to live in Your courts! Let them be filled with the good things of Your house (Ps. 65:4, NIV).

Answer me with awesome deeds of righteousness (Ps. 65:5).

Still the roaring of the seas, the roaring of their waves, and the turmoil of the nations (Ps. 65:7).

Care for the land and water it; enrich it abundantly from the streams of God that are filled with water to provide the people with grain. Drench its furrows and level its ridges; soften it with showers and bless its crops (Ps. 65:9–10, NIV).

Crown the year with Your bounty, and let Your paths drip with abundance; drop on the pastures of the wilderness, and the little hills will rejoice on every side (Ps. 65:11–12).

Let the pastures be clothed with flocks, and the valleys also be covered with grain; let them shout for joy and sing (Ps. 65:13).

Make a joyful shout to God, all the earth (Ps. 66:1).

Sing out the honor of His name; make His praise glorious (Ps. 66:2).

How awesome are Your works! Through the greatness of Your power Your enemies shall submit themselves to You (Ps. 66:3).

Let all the earth worship You and sing unto You; they will sing praises to Your name (Ps. 66:4).

Lord, rule by Your power forever, and let Your eyes observe the nations; do not let the rebellious exalt themselves (Ps. 66:7).

Lord, bring me into a place of abundance (Ps. 66:12).

Let God arise, let His enemies be scattered; let those also who hate Him flee before Him (Ps. 68:1).

I will be glad and rejoice before my God, and I will exceedingly rejoice (Ps. 68:3).

Let the nations sing unto God, "Our God, You are the one who rides on the clouds, and we praise You. Your name is the Lord, and we celebrate as we worship You" (Ps. 68:4, CEV).

Lord, set the lonely in families, and lead forth the prisoners with singing; but let the rebellious live in a sun-scorched land (Ps. 68:6, NIV).

The earth trembled, the heavens also poured down [rain] at the presence of God. You, O God, did send a plentiful rain; You did restore and confirm Your heritage when it languished and was weary (Ps. 68:8–9, AMP).

Lord, give the word, and let a great company publish it (Ps. 68:11).

Sing to God, you kingdoms of the earth; oh, sing praises to the Lord (Ps. 68:32).

You have saved Zion and built the cities of Judah [praise]. I will dwell in Zion and have it in possession (Ps. 69:35).

I inherit Zion; I dwell in Zion because I love Your name (Ps. 69:36).

In You, O Lord, I put my trust; let me never be put to shame (Ps. 71:1).

I have become as a wonder to many, but You are my strong refuge (Ps. 71:7).

I will go in the strength of the Lord God; I will make mention of Your righteousness, of Yours only (Ps. 71:16).

Lord, increase my greatness, and comfort me on every side (Ps. 71:21).

Let the mountains bring peace [shalom] to the people, and the hills, through [the general establishment of] righteousness (Ps. 72:3, AMP).

Lord, bring justice to the poor of the people; save the children of the needy, and break in pieces the oppressor (Ps. 72:4).

Let the nations fear You as long as the sun and moon endure, throughout all generations (Ps. 72:5).

Lord, come down as rain upon the mown grass, as showers that water the earth (Ps. 72:6).

Lord, I live in the days of the kingdom; let the righteous flourish and have abundance of peace [*shalom*], until the moon is no more (Ps. 72:7).

Let Your dominion be from sea to sea, and from the River to the ends of the earth (Ps. 72:8).

Let those in the wilderness bow before You, Lord, and let Your enemies lick the dust (Ps. 72:9).

Let the kings of Tarshish and Sheba offer gifts (Ps. 72:10).

Let all kings bow down, and let all nations serve You (Ps. 72:11).

Lord, deliver the needy when they cry, and the poor who have no helper. Spare the poor and needy, and spare the souls of the needy (Ps. 72:12–13).

Your name will endure forever, and Your name shall continue as long as the sun. Men will be blessed in You, and all nations will call You blessed (Ps. 72:17).

Blessed be Your glorious name forever! Let the whole earth be filled with Your glory (Ps. 72:19).

Crush the heads of Leviathan, and give him as food for the creatures inhabiting the wilderness (Ps. 74:14, AMP).

Cut off the horns of the wicked, and let the horns of the righteous be exalted (Ps. 75:10).

Cut off the spirit [of pride and fury] of princes; You are terrible to the [ungodly] kings of the earth (Ps. 76:12).

Let the groaning of the prisoner come before You; according to the greatness of Your power preserve those who are appointed to die (Ps. 79:11).

The haters of the Lord will pretend submission to You, but their fate will endure forever (Ps. 81:15).

Let men know that You, whose name is Jehovah, are the Most High over all the earth (Ps. 83:18).

I will go from strength to strength and appear before You, Lord, in Zion (Ps. 84:7).

Lord, You are a sun and shield; You give grace and glory; no good thing will You withhold from those who walk uprightly (Ps. 84:11).

Lord, You have been favorable to me and brought back my captivity; You have forgiven my iniquity and covered all my sin (Ps. 85:1–2).

Let truth spring out of the earth, and let righteousness look down from heaven (Ps. 85:11).

Let all nations come and worship before You, O Lord, and let them glorify Your name (Ps. 86:9).

Show that You approve of me! Then my hateful enemies will feel like fools, because You have helped and comforted me (Ps. 86:17, CEV).

Lord, You love the gates of Zion [the church], and glorious things are spoken of Zion, the city of God (Ps. 87:2–3).

Lord, I am born in Zion; let Zion be established in all the earth (Ps. 87:5).

You will satisfy me with long life and show me Your salvation (Ps. 91:16).

My horn (emblem of excessive strength and stately grace) You have exalted like that of a wild ox; I am anointed with fresh oil (Ps. 92:10, AMP).

I will flourish like the palm tree and grow like a cedar in Lebanon (Ps. 92:12).

I am planted in the house of the Lord and flourish in the courts of my God (Ps. 92:13).

I am [growing in grace] and will still bring forth fruit in old age; I will be full of sap [of spiritual vitality] and [rich in the] verdure [of trust, love, and contentment] (Ps. 92:14, AMP).

The Lord reigns, He is clothed with majesty; the Lord is robed, He has girded Himself with strength and power; the world also is established, that it cannot be moved (Ps. 93:1, AMP).

Lord, subdue the floods that have lifted up, for You are mightier than the noise of many waters (Ps. 93:3–4).

I will sing unto the Lord a new song. Let the earth sing unto the Lord (Ps. 96:1).

I will proclaim the good news of Your salvation from day to day (Ps. 96:2).

I will declare Your glory among the nations, and Your wonders among all people (Ps. 96:3).

Let the families of the peoples give to the Lord glory and strength. Let them give to the Lord the glory due His name; let them bring an offering and come into His courts (Ps. 96:7–8).

Let the nations worship the Lord in the beauty of holiness, and fear before Him (Ps. 96:9).

Let the earth be firmly established, and let the nations say, "The Lord reigns" (Ps. 96:10).

Let the heavens rejoice, let the earth be glad; let the sea resound, and all that is in it (Ps. 96:11, NIV).

Let the fields be jubilant, and everything in them. Then all the trees of the forest will sing for joy (Ps. 96:12).

Lord, You reign. Let the earth rejoice; let the multitude of the islands be glad (Ps. 97:1).

Let the heavens declare Your righteousness, and all the people see Your glory (Ps. 97:6).

I will sing unto You a new song, for You have done marvelous things (Ps. 98:1).

Lord, make Your salvation known, and reveal Your righteousness to the nations (Ps. 98:2).

Shout for joy to the Lord, all the earth; burst into jubilant song with music (Ps. 98:4).

Let the sea resound, and everything in it; the world, and all who live in it (Ps. 98:7).

Let the rivers clap their hands, let the mountains sing together for joy; let them sing before the Lord (Ps. 98:8–9, NIV).

Lord, You reign; let the people tremble, for You are great in Zion (Ps. 99:1–2).

Lord, Your word says that it is the set, appointed time to favor Zion. As a citizen of Zion, I declare that I walk in the favor of God. It is the appointed time for Your favor to abound and increase toward me (Ps. 102:13).

Lord, build up Zion and appear in Your glory, so the nations can fear You, and all the kings of the earth see Your glory (Ps. 102:15–16).

Lord, You will hear the prayer of the destitute, and You will not despise their prayer (Ps. 102:17).

Lord, You will look down from the height of Your sanctuary and will hear the groaning of the prisoner and will release those appointed to death (Ps. 102:19–20).

I will praise the Lord from my inmost being, and I will forget not all His benefits (Ps. 103:2).

Lord, You forgive all my sins and heal all my diseases (Ps. 103:3, NIV).

Lord, You have redeemed my life from the pit, and You have crowned me with love and compassion (Ps. 103:4, NIV).

You satisfy my desires with good things, so that my youth is renewed like the eagle's (Ps. 103:5).

Lord, work righteousness and justice for all the oppressed (Ps. 103:6, NIV).

As far as the east is from the west, so far have You removed my transgression from me (Ps. 103:12).

Lord, You have established Your throne in heaven, and Your kingdom rules over all (Ps. 103:19).

All of God's creation and all that He rules, come and praise the Lord! With all my heart I praise the Lord! (Ps. 103:22).

How many are your works, O Lord! In wisdom You made them all; the earth is full of Your creatures (Ps. 104:24, NIV).

May the glory of the Lord endure forever; may the Lord rejoice in his works (Ps. 104:31, NIV).

Lord, turn my desert into pools of water and my parched ground into flowing springs (Ps. 107:35, NIV).

Lord, send forth from Zion the scepter of Your strength; rule, then, in the midst of Your foes (Ps. 110:2, AMP).

Lord, give me meat, and be ever mindful of Your covenant (Ps. 111:5).

Lord, You sent redemption to Your people, and You have commanded Your covenant forever; holy and reverent is Your name (Ps. 111:9).

From the rising of the sun to its going down, the Lord's name is to be praised. The Lord is high above all nations, His glory above the heavens (Ps. 113:3–4).

Raise the poor out of the dust, and lift the needy out of the ash heap (Ps. 113:7).

Grant the barren woman a home, like a joyful mother of children (Ps. 113:9).

Tremble, O earth, at the presence of the Lord, at the presence of the God of Jacob (Ps. 114:7).

All of you nations, come praise the Lord! Let everyone praise Him. His love for us is wonderful; His faithfulness never ends. Shout praises to the Lord! (Ps. 117).

Shouts of joy and victory resound in the tents of the righteous: "The Lord's right hand has done mighty things!" (Ps. 118:15).

Lord, You have opened the gates of righteousness; I will go into them, and I will praise You (Ps. 118:19).

The stone which the builders rejected has become the chief cornerstone. This was the Lord's doing; it is marvelous in my eyes (Ps. 118:22–23).

This is the day You have made; I will rejoice and be glad in it (Ps. 118:24).

Save now, we beseech You, O Lord; send now prosperity, O Lord, we beseech You, and give to us success! (Ps. 118:25, AMP).

The Lord is your keeper; the Lord is your shade at your right hand. The sun shall not strike you by day, nor the moon by night. The Lord shall preserve you from all evil; He shall preserve your soul (Ps. 121:5–7).

The Lord will preserve my going out and my coming in from this time forth, and even forevermore (Ps. 121:8).

Let peace [*shalom*] be within my walls, and prosperity within my palace (Ps. 122:7).

Lord, surround Your people as the mountains surround Jerusalem, from this time forth and forever (Ps. 125:2).

Let Your priests be clothed with righteousness, and let Your saints shout for joy (Ps. 132:9).

Lord, You have chosen Zion [Your church] and have desired it for Your dwelling place. This is

Your resting place forever; here You dwell, for You have desired it (Ps. 132:13–14).

Bless my provision, and satisfy me with bread (Ps. 132:15).

Clothe me with salvation, and I will shout aloud for joy (Ps. 132:16).

Lord, command Your blessing upon Zion [the church], even life forevermore (Ps. 133:3).

I will lift up my hands in the sanctuary, and I will bless the Lord. Lord, You made heaven and earth, and you will bless me out of Zion (Ps. 134:2–3).

Lord, Your mercy endures forever (Ps. 136).

Let all the kings of the earth praise You when they hear the words of Your mouth (Ps. 138:4).

Lord, perfect that which concerns me, for Your mercy endures forever (Ps. 138:8).

I will praise You, O Lord, for I am fearfully and wonderfully made (Ps. 139:14).

Lord, Your thoughts are precious unto me; how great is the sum of them! They are more in number than the sand (Ps. 139:17–18).

Set a guard, O Lord, over my mouth; keep watch over the door of my lips (Ps. 141:3).

I pray to you, Lord! You are my place of safety, and You are my choice in the land of the living. Please answer my prayer. I am completely helpless. Help! They are chasing me, and they are too strong. Rescue me from this prison, so I can praise Your name. And when Your people notice Your wonderful kindness to me, they will rush to my side (Ps. 142:5–7, CEV).

Cause me to hear Your lovingkindness in the morning, for in You do I trust; cause me to know the way in which I should walk, for I lift up my soul to You (Ps. 143:8).

Teach me to do Your will, for You are my God; Your Spirit is good. Lead me in the land of uprightness (Ps. 143:10).

Lord, You are my steadfast love and my fortress, my high tower and my deliverer, my shield and He in whom I trust and take refuge, who subdues my people under me (Ps. 144:2).

Let our sons be as plants grown up in their youth (Ps. 144:12).

Let our daughters be as pillars, sculptured in palace style (Ps. 144:12).

Let our barns be full, supplying all kinds of produce (Ps. 144:13).

Let our sheep bring forth thousands and ten thousands in our fields (Ps. 144:13).

Let our oxen be strong to labor; that there be no breaking in or going out; that there be no complaining in our streets. Happy am I, whose God is the Lord (Ps. 144:14–15).

Let this generation praise Your works to the next, and declare Your mighty acts (Ps. 145:4).

I will meditate on the glorious splendor of Your majesty, and on Your wondrous works (Ps. 145:5).

Men shall speak of the might of Your awesome acts, and I will declare Your greatness (Ps. 145:6).

Let men speak of the glory of Your kingdom and talk of Your power (Ps. 145:11).

Your kingdom is an everlasting kingdom, and Your dominion endures throughout all generations (Ps. 145:13).

Lord, give freedom to the prisoners (Ps. 146:7).

Lord, open the eyes of the blind, and raise up those who are bowed down (Ps. 146:8).

Lord, watch over the strangers and relieve the fatherless and widow, but turn the way of the wicked upside down (Ps. 146:9).

Let Your kingdom and reign touch this generation (Ps. 146:10).

Lord, build up Jerusalem [Your church], and gather together the outcasts of Israel (Ps. 147:2).

Lord, heal the brokenhearted, and bind up their wounds (Ps. 147:3).

Lord, lift up the humble, but cast the wicked to the ground (Ps. 147:6).

Lord, make peace within my borders, and fill me with the finest of wheat (Ps. 147:14).

Let the heavens, the heights, the angels, the sun, the moon, and stars of light praise You, Lord. Let the heavens of heavens, the waters above the heavens, praise the name of the Lord: for He commanded, and they were created (Ps. 148:1–5).

Praise the Lord from the earth, you great sea creatures and all the depths; fire and hail, snow and clouds; stormy wind, fulfilling His word; mountains and all hills; fruitful trees and all cedars; beasts and all cattle; creeping things and flying fowl; kings of the earth and all peoples; princes and all judges of the earth; both young men and maidens; old men and children. Let them praise the name of the Lord, for His name alone is exalted; His glory is above the earth and heaven (Ps. 148:7–13).

Praise the Lord! Sing to the Lord a new song, and His praise in the assembly of saints (Ps. 149:1).

I will rejoice in Him who made me. Let Zion be joyful in their King (Ps. 149:2).

Lord, take pleasure in me, and beautify me with salvation (Ps. 149:4).

Where the word of a king is, there is power; Lord, release Your word (Eccles. 8:4).

Let the nations come to the mountain of the house of the Lord [the church], and let them learn His ways and walk in His paths. Let them beat their swords into plowshares, and their spears into pruninghooks, and let them learn war no more (Isa. 2:2–4).

Let the people who walk in darkness and in the shadow of death see Your light (Isa. 9:2).

Of the increase of Your government and peace [*shalom*], there is no end. Let Your government and peace increase from generation to generation (Isa. 9:7).

Let Your remnant, Your elect, depend on You, the Holy One of Israel. Let Your remnant return to You as the sand of the sea, for the destruction decreed shall overflow with righteousness (Isa. 10:20–22).

Lord, You are the root of Jesse, and You stand as a banner to Your people. Let the nations seek You and enter into Your glorious rest (Isa. 11:10).

God is my salvation. I will trust and not be afraid, for the Lord Jehovah is my strength and my song; He has become my salvation (Isa. 12:2).

With joy will I draw water from the wells of salvation (Isa. 12:3).

I will praise the Lord, call upon His name, declare His doings among the people, and make mention that His name is exalted (Isa. 12:4).

I will sing unto the Lord, for He has done excellent things; this is known in all the earth (Isa. 12:5).

I will cry out and shout, because I am an inhabitant of Zion, and great is the Holy One of Israel in my midst (Isa. 12:6).

Let me enjoy the rest I have in Christ. I have rest from sorrow and from fear and from hard bondage (Isa. 14:3).

The whole earth [the church] is at rest and is quiet; let them [the church] break forth into singing (Isa. 14:7).

Let the trees [the church] rejoice at the fall of the oppressor (Isa. 14:8).

Lord, exactly as You planned, it will happen. These are Your blueprints, it will take shape. You will shatter the enemies who trespass on Your land and will stomp them into the dirt on Your mountains. You will ban them from taking and making slaves of Your people and will lift the weight of oppression from all shoulders. This is Your plan, planned for the whole earth. And it is Your hand that will do it, reaching into every nation. God-of-the-Angel-Armies has planned it. Who could ever cancel such plans? Your hand has reached out. Who could brush it aside? (Isa. 14:24–27, The Message).

Lord, Your throne is established in mercy, and You sit upon it in truth in the tabernacle of David, judging and seeking justice and hastening righteousness (Isa. 16:5).

Lord, on Mount [Zion] You will make for all peoples a feast of rich things [symbolic of Your coronation festival inaugurating the reign of the Lord on earth, in the wake of a background of gloom, judgment, and terror], a feast of wines on the lees—of fat things full of marrow, of wines on the lees well refined. And You will destroy on this mountain the covering of the face that is cast over the heads of all peoples [in mourning], and the veil [of profound wretchedness] that is woven and spread over all nations (Isa. 25:6–7, AMP).

Lord, I sing a new song. I have a strong city; salvation is appointed for walls and bulwarks (Isa. 26:1).

The gates of Zion are opened; let the righteous nation that keeps Your truth enter (Isa. 26:2).

You will keep me in perfect peace, because my mind is stayed on You, and I trust in You (Isa. 26:3).

I will trust in the Lord forever; for in the Lord Jehovah is everlasting strength (Isa. 26:4).

Lord, You will establish peace [*shalom*] for us (Isa. 26:12).

You will [deliver Israel from her enemies and also from the rebel powers of evil and darkness]. Your sharp and unrelenting, great, and strong sword will visit and punish Leviathan the swiftly fleeing serpent, Leviathan the twisting and winding serpent (Isa. 27:1, AMP).

I will sing the song of Your church, a fruitful vineyard. You will water me every moment, and guard me night and day so that no one may harm me (Isa. 27:2–3).

Lord, You have laid a stone in Zion [Your church] and placed it for a foundation, a stone, a tried stone, a precious cornerstone, a sure foundation, and I will never be dismayed because I trust You (Isa. 28:16).

Lord, You long to be gracious to me; You rise to show me compassion. You are a God of justice. I will wait for You and be blessed (Isa. 30:18, NIV).

I hear the voice of the Lord. He tells me the way, when I should turn to the right, or to the left, and counsels me to walk in the way (Isa. 30:21).

I have a song, and gladness of heart, and I come to the mountain of the Lord, to the Mighty One of Israel (Isa. 30:29).

Let Your Spirit be poured out from on high, and the wilderness be a fruitful field, and the fruitful field be counted for a forest (Isa. 32:15).

Let righteousness work peace in my life, and let the effect of righteousness be quietness and confidence forever (Isa. 32:17, NIV).

Let me dwell in a peaceful dwelling place, and in secure homes, in undisturbed places of rest (Isa. 32:18, NIV).

Lord, be gracious to me; I long for you. Be my strength every morning, my salvation in time of distress (Isa. 33:2, NIV).

Let wisdom and knowledge be my stability, and strength of salvation, and the fear of the Lord my treasure (Isa. 33:6).

Lord, I will walk righteously and speak uprightly; I will despise gain from fraud and from oppression, and will shake my hand free from the taking of bribes; I will stop my ears from hearing of bloodshed and shut my eyes to avoid looking upon evil. Therefore You will cause me to dwell on the heights; my place of defense will be the fortresses of rocks; bread will be given to me, and water for me will be sure (Isa. 33:15–16, NIV).

Let my eyes see Your beauty, Lord (Isa. 33:17).

Let Your church be as secure as a tent with pegs that cannot be pulled up and fastened with ropes that can never be broken (Isa. 33:20, CEV).

Lord, be unto me a place of broad rivers and streams (Isa. 33:21).

I will not say I am sick, because my iniquity is forgiven (Isa. 33:24).

Let every wilderness and solitary place in my life rejoice, and blossom abundantly as a rose (Isa. 35:1).

Let rejoicing, joy, and singing come into every wilderness place (Isa. 35:2).

Let the glory of Lebanon, the excellence of Carmel and Sharon, come into my life, and let me see the glory of the Lord (Isa. 35:2).

Strengthen my weak hands, and make firm my feeble knees (Isa. 35:3).

Let my eyes be opened, and every blind area of my life be removed (Isa. 35:5).

Let my ears be opened, and let every deaf area of life be unstopped (Isa. 35:5).

Let every lame area of my life be healed, and let me leap like a deer (Isa. 35:6).

Let my tongue sing for joy, and let waters and streams break out in every area of my life (Isa. 35:6).

Let every parched area of my life become a pool, and every thirsty area of my life a spring of water (Isa. 35:7).

Let me walk on the highway of holiness, and let no lion or ravenous beast be in my path, for I am the redeemed of the Lord (Isa. 35:8–9).

I will come to Zion with songs and everlasting joy upon my head (Isa. 35:10).

I will obtain joy and gladness, and sorrow and sighing will flee from my life (Isa. 35:10).

I receive the comfort of the Lord, my iniquity is pardoned, and my warfare is accomplished (Isa. 40:1–2).

The way of the LORD is made straight in my life, and a highway has been made in my life for my God (Isa. 40:3).

Let every valley in my life be exalted, and every mountain be made low (Isa. 40:4).

Lord, make the crooked places in my life straight, and every rough place smooth (Isa. 40:4).

Let the glory of the Lord be revealed in my life, for You, Lord, have spoken it (Isa. 40:5).

I will go to the mountain of the Lord, and I will lift up my voice with strength and declare, "Behold your God!" (Isa. 40:9).

Lord, I am a part of Your flock; feed me, and gently lead me (Isa. 40:11).

Lord, give me power and increase my strength. (Isa. 40:29).

I will wait upon the Lord and renew my strength. (Isa. 40:31).

I will mount up with wings as an eagle; I will run and not be weary, I will walk and not be faint. (Isa. 40:31).

Lord, I will not fear, for You are with me; You strengthen me, help me, and uphold me with Your righteous right hand (Isa. 41:10).

I will not fear, for You, Lord, will hold my hand and help me (Isa. 41:13).

Lord, You have allowed me to become like a log covered with sharp spikes. You will help me to grind and crush every mountain and hill until they turn to dust. A strong wind will scatter them in all directions (Isa. 41:15–16, CEV).

Lord, open rivers in high places for me, and fountains in the midst of my valley (Isa. 41:18).

Lord, in every desert place in my life, You will fill the desert with all kinds of trees—cedars, acacias, and myrtles; olive and cypress trees; fir trees and pines (Isa. 41:19).

Everyone will see and know, and consider and understand together, that the hand of the Lord has done this in my life, and that I am Your new creation (Isa. 41:20).

Lord, establish Your justice in the earth, and let the coastlands receive Your law (Isa. 42:4).

Let the blind eyes be opened, bring out the prisoners from prison, and those that sit in darkness out of the prison house (Isa. 42:7).

Let new things be declared in my life, and let them spring forth (Isa. 42:9).

I will sing unto You a new song and release Your praise from my life (Isa. 42:10).

Let the wilderness areas in my life lift up their voices, and let me shout from the top of the mountains (Isa. 42:11).

I will give You glory and declare Your praise (Isa. 42:12).

Lord, go forth as a mighty man; cry, roar, and prevail against Your enemies (Isa. 42:13).

Lord, bring the blind by a way they know not, and lead them in paths they have not known. (Isa. 42:16).

Make darkness light before me, and crooked things straight in my life (Isa. 42:16).

Lord, magnify Your law, and make it honorable (Isa. 42:21).

Lord, You have redeemed me; You have summoned me by name; I am Yours. I will not be afraid (Isa. 43:1, NIV).

When I pass through the waters, You will be with me; the rivers will not overflow my life (Isa. 43:2).

When I walk through the fire, I will not be burned, and the flames will not set me ablaze (Isa. 43:2).

Lord, You have brought me from the ends of the earth and joined me to the Holy One of Israel (Isa. 43:3–6).

Lord, You have created me for Your glory; You have formed me and made me (Isa. 43:7).

Lord, I am Your witness, I am Your servant, You have chosen me, and there is no other God beside You (Isa. 43:10–11).

Lord, make a way in the sea and a path in the mighty waters (Isa. 43:16).

Lord, You drew out the chariots and horses, the army and reinforcements together, and they lay there, never to rise again, extinguished, snuffed out like a wick (Isa. 43:17, NIV).

Lord, help me to forget the former things and not to dwell on the past. Do a new thing in my life. Make a way in the wilderness and rivers in the desert (Isa. 43:19).

Let the wild animals of the field honor You, the jackals and the owls, because You provide water in the wilderness and streams in the wasteland to give drink to me, Your chosen (Isa. 43:20).

Lord, You have formed me for Yourself, and I will show forth Your praise (Isa. 43:21).

Lord, You have blotted out my sins for Your sake, and You will not remember my sins (Isa. 43:25).

Pour water upon every thirsty place of my life and floods upon every dry place in my life (Isa. 44:3).

Pour Your spirit on my descendants and blessing upon my offspring (Isa. 44:3, NIV).

Let my offspring spring up like grass or like willow trees near flowing streams to worship You and to be Your people (Isa. 44:4, NIV).

You have swept away my offenses like a cloud, like the morning mist. I have returned to You, for You have redeemed me (Isa. 44:22, NIV).

Let the heavens sing, and let the lower parts of the earth shout, for the Lord has done this (Isa. 44:23, NIV).

Let the mountains, the forest, and every tree sing, for the Lord has redeemed me (Isa. 44:23, NIV).

Lord, foil the signs of false prophets and make fools of diviners; overthrow the learning of the wise and turn it into nonsense (Isa. 44:25, NIV).

Carry out the words of Your servants, and fulfill the predictions of Your messengers (Isa. 44:26, NIV).

Let Jerusalem, Your church, be inhabited, let the cities of Judah (praise) be built, and let the decayed places be restored (Isa. 44:26, NIV).

Let the deep be dry, and dry up the rivers, that Your anointed may cross over (Isa. 44:27–28, NIV).

Lord, I am Your anointed. Take me by the right hand, and subdue nations, strip kings of their armor, and open doors before me so that gates will not be shut (Isa. 45:1, NIV).

Go before me, and level the mountains, break the gates of brass, and cut through the bars of iron (Isa. 45:2, NIV).

Give me the treasures of darkness and hidden riches of secret places (Isa. 45:3, NIV).

Let the heavens rain down, and the skies pour down righteousness. Let the earth open and bring forth salvation, and let righteousness spring up together (Isa. 45:8).

Let the nations come and fall down, saying, "God is in you, and there is no other god" (Isa. 45:14).

I am saved with an everlasting salvation, and the Lord will always keep me safe and free from shame (Isa. 45:17, CEV).

Let the ends of the earth look unto You and be saved (Isa. 45:22).

In the Lord I have righteousness and strength (Isa. 45:24).

I am justified in the Lord, and I glory in His salvation (Isa. 45:25).

Let every idol bow and stoop before the Lord (Isa. 46:1).

Lord, You declare the end from the beginning. Let Your counsel stand, and do all Your pleasure (Isa. 46:10).

Lord, You have placed Your righteousness and salvation in Zion (Isa. 46:13).

Teach me to profit, and lead me in the way I should go (Isa. 48:17).

Lord, You are a light to the nations, and Your salvation goes to the ends of the earth (Isa. 49:6).

Let kings see You and arise; let princes fall down and worship, because You are faithful and have chosen me (Isa. 49:7).

Lord, You have said that You will answer my prayers and have set a time when You will come to save me. You have chosen me to take Your promise of hope to other nations. You will rebuild the country from its ruins, and then people will come and settle there (Isa. 49:8, CEV).

You will set prisoners free from dark dungeons to see the light of day. On their way home, they will find plenty to eat, even on barren hills. They won't go hungry or get thirsty; they won't be bothered by the scorching sun or hot desert winds. You will be merciful while leading them along to streams of water (Isa. 49:9–10, CEV).

Let Your mountains become a way, and let Your highways be exalted (Isa. 49:11).

Shout for joy, O heavens; rejoice, O earth; burst into song, O mountains! For the Lord comforts His people and will have compassion on His afflicted ones (Isa. 49:13, NIV).

Let our children make haste, and let the destroyers go forth out of my life (Isa. 49:17).

Lord, thank You for Your promise to signal all the nations to return our sons and our daughters to the arms of Jerusalem [the church] (Isa. 49:22, CEV).

Let kings and queens bow down to You, and let those who wait for You not be ashamed (Isa. 49:23).

Let the captives of the mighty be taken away and the prey of the terrible be delivered (Isa. 49:25).

Lord, You have comforted Zion [the church] and looked with compassion on all her ruins (Isa. 51:3, NIV).

Lord, cause my desert places to be like the Garden of Eden, and my wastelands like the garden of the Lord. Fill me with joy and gladness, thanksgiving, and the sound of singing (Isa. 51:3, NIV).

Lord, was it not You who dried up the sea, the waters of the great deep, who made a road in the depths of the sea so that the redeemed might cross over? (Isa. 51:10, NIV).

You have ransomed me and caused me to enter Zion with singing; You have given me a crown of everlasting joy and gladness, and sorrow and sighing will flee away (Isa. 51:11, NIV).

Lord, You have put Your words in my mouth and covered me with the shadow of Your hand, that You might plant the heavens, lay the foundations of the earth, and say unto Zion, "You are My people" (Isa. 51:16).

I will awake, put on strength, and put on my beautiful garments, and nothing unclean will come through my life (Isa. 52:1).

I shake myself and loose myself from the bands of my neck, for I am redeemed without money (Isa. 52:2–3).

Let the gospel of the kingdom be preached; let the good tidings of peace be published; I will declare, "My God reigns" (Isa. 52:7).

Let the waste places break forth into joy and sing together, for You have comforted Your people (Isa. 52:9).

Make bare Your holy arm in the eyes of all nations, and let the ends of the earth see Your salvation (Isa. 52:10).

Lord, go before me and be my rear guard (Isa. 52:12).

Lord, sprinkle many nations; let them see, and those who have not heard, let them consider (Isa. 52:15).

I have believed Your report, and Your arm is revealed unto me (Isa. 53:1).

Lord, You have borne my griefs and carried my sorrows; You were wounded for my transgressions and bruised for my iniquities; the chastisement for my peace was upon You, and by Your stripes I am healed (Isa. 53:4–5).

I will sing and shout for joy, for You have told me to enlarge the place of my tent and to stretch my tent curtains wide, for my descendants will dispossess nations and settle in their desolate cities (Isa. 54:1–3, NIV).

I will not be afraid and I will not be ashamed, for the LORD is my maker, and He is the God of the whole earth (Isa. 54:5).

Lord, though the mountains be shaken and the hills be removed, Your unfailing love for me will not be shaken and Your covenant of peace will not be removed from my life, for You have had compassion on me (Isa. 54:10, NIV).

Although I have been lashed by storms, You have promised to build me with stones of turquoise and my foundations with sapphires. You will make battlements for me of rubies and gates of sparkling jewels and all my walls of precious stones (Isa. 54:11–12, NIV).

I am taught of the LORD, and I have great peace [*shalom*] (Isa. 54:13).

I am established in righteousness, and tyranny will be far from me; I will have nothing to fear, for terror will be far removed and will not come near me (Isa. 54:14, NIV).

No weapon forged against me will prevail, and I will refute every tongue that accuses me, for this is my heritage and my vindication from the Lord (Isa. 54:17, NIV).

I receive the everlasting covenant, and I receive the sure mercies of David (Isa. 55:3).

I go out with joy, and I am led forth with peace; the mountains and the hills break forth before me into singing, and all the trees of the field clap their hands (Isa. 55:12).

Cypress and myrtle trees will grow in fields once covered by thorns. And then those trees will stand as a lasting witness to the glory of the Lord (Isa. 55:13, CEV).

Lord, You have given me a place within Your walls, and You have given me a name, an everlasting name, that shall not be cut off (Isa. 56:5).

I have come to the mountain of the Lord, and I am joyful in the house of prayer, and I offer to God the sacrifices of praise (Isa. 56:7).

Lord, let my light break forth as the morning, let my health spring forth speedily, let my righteousness go before me, and let You, Lord, be my rear guard (Isa. 58:8).

Lord, guide me continually, and satisfy my soul in drought, and strengthen my bones; let me be like a watered garden and like a spring of water, whose waters fail not (Isa. 58:11).

Lord, let me build up the old waste places, and let me raise up the foundations of many generations; let me be the repairer of the breach and the restorer of paths to dwell in (Isa. 58:12, KJV).

Lord, I delight in You; cause me to ride upon the high places of the earth, and feed me with the heritage of Jacob, for Your mouth has spoken it (Isa. 58:14).

Let the nations fear You from the west, and Your glory from the rising of the sun (Isa. 59:19).

When the enemy comes in like a flood, the Spirit of the Lord shall lift up a standard against him (Isa. 59:19).

Lord, I receive Your covenant, and Your Spirit is upon me, and Your words are in my mouth (Isa. 59:21).

Let Your church arise and shine, for the glory of the Lord is risen upon us (Isa. 60:1).

Let the glory of the Lord be seen upon the church, and let those in darkness come to the light, and see the brightness of our rising (Isa. 60:2–3).

Let the sons and daughters of the nations come to Zion (Isa. 60:4).

Let our hearts swell with joy, because the abundance of the sea shall be turned to us, and the wealth of the Gentiles shall come to Zion [the church] (Isa. 60:5).

Zion's gates are open continually; they are not shut day or night, that men may bring the wealth of the nations (Isa. 60:11).

Let the glory of Lebanon come to Zion, let Your sanctuary be beautified, and let the place of Your feet be glorious (Isa. 60:13).

We are the city of the Lord, the Zion of the Holy One of Israel (Isa. 60:14).

Lord, [instead of the tyranny of the present] You will appoint peace as your officers and righteousness as your taskmasters (Isa. 60:17, AMP).

Violence shall no more be heard in my land, nor devastation or destruction within my borders, but I will call my walls Salvation and my gates Praise (Isa. 60:18, AMP).

The Lord is my everlasting light, and my God is my glory (Isa. 60:19).

Lord, this is what You have promised: "Your sun will never set or your moon go down. I, the

Lord, will be your everlasting light, and your days of sorrow will come to an end. Your people will live right and always own the land; they are the trees I planted to bring praise to me. Even the smallest family will be a powerful nation," for You are the Lord, and when the time comes, You will quickly accomplish Your Word (Isa. 60:20–22, CEV).

Lord, You give me beauty for ashes, the oil of joy for mourning, the garment of praise for the spirit of heaviness; that I may be called a tree of righteousness, Your planting, that You may be glorified (Isa. 61:3).

I am a priest of the Lord, a servant of God, and I eat the riches of the nations (Isa. 61:6).

Instead of shame, I will receive double honor (Isa. 61:7).

I receive the everlasting covenant, and I am the seed that the Lord has blessed (Isa. 61:8–9).

I delight greatly in the Lord; my soul rejoices in my God. For he has clothed me with garments of salvation and arrayed me in a robe of righteousness (Isa. 61:10, NIV).

Let righteousness and praise spring forth before all nations (Isa. 61:11).

Let the nations see Your righteousness, and all kings Your glory (Isa. 62:2).

I am a crown of glory in the hand of the Lord, and a royal diadem in the hand of my God (Isa. 62:3).

I [Judah] will no more be termed Forsaken, nor shall my land be called Desolate any more. I will be called Hephzibah [My delight is in her], and my land be called Beulah [married]; for the Lord delights in me, and my land shall be married [owned and protected by the Lord] (Isa. 62:4, AMP).

I will give You no rest until Jerusalem [the church] is established and made a praise in the earth (Isa. 62:7).

I will eat and drink in the courts of Your holiness (Isa. 62:9, KJV).

I am the redeemed of the Lord, and I am sought out, a city not forsaken (Isa. 62:12).

I will mention the loving-kindnesses of the Lord and the praises of the Lord, according to all that the Lord has bestowed on me, and the great goodness toward the house of Israel [the church], which He has bestowed on them according to His mercies, according to the multitude of His loving-kindnesses (Isa. 63:7).

Since ancient times no one has heard, no ear has perceived, no eye has seen any God besides You, who acts on behalf of those who wait for Him. But You, Lord, have revealed them unto me by Your Spirit (Isa. 64:4, NIV; 1 Cor. 2:10).

Lord, meet me as I rejoice and work righteousness (Isa. 64:5).

Lord, You are the potter, and I am the clay; I am the work of Your hand (Isa. 64:8).

I am the seed of Jacob. I am the elect, and I inherit the holy mountains and dwell there (Isa. 65:9).

I dwell in Sharon and lie down in the valley of Achor (Isa. 65:10).

I am a new creation in Christ, and my former life is not remembered, nor does it come into mind (Isa. 65:17).

I will be glad and rejoice in the new creation, for You have created Your church a rejoicing, and Your people a joy (Isa. 65:18).

Lord, You rejoice over me, and weeping and crying has departed from my life (Isa. 65:19).

I will not labor in vain, but I will enjoy the fruit of my labor, for I am the blessed of the Lord (Isa. 65:21–23).

Before I call, You will answer; and while I am yet speaking, You will hear (Isa. 65:24).

You have caused the Jew and Gentile [wolf and lamb] to feed together in Your church, and the dust is the serpent's meat. There is no hurt or destruction in Your holy mountain (Isa. 65:25).

Rejoice in Jerusalem [the church], and be glad with her, all you who love her. Rejoice for joy with her, all you who mourn for her (Isa. 66:10).

Lord, extend peace [*shalom*] to Your church like a river (Isa. 66:12).

My heart rejoices and my bones flourish like an herb, and the hand of the Lord is made known to me (Isa. 66:14).

I come to the mountain of the Lord, to Zion, and I offer myself as a living sacrifice (Isa. 66:20).

I am a priest and a Levite because of the new covenant, and the new creation, and I am a worshiper (Isa. 66:21–23).

Lord, I trust in You. Let me be as a tree planted by the waters that spreads my roots by the river, so I need not fear when heat comes. Let my leaf be green, and keep me worry-free in the year of drought, never failing to bear fruit (Jer. 17:7–8, NIV).

Lord, You are the branch of David; reign and prosper, and execute judgment and justice in the earth (Jer. 23:5).

You are the Lord our righteousness; I am saved, and I dwell safely (Jer. 23:6).

You have redeemed me and ransomed me from those who are stronger than me (Jer. 31:11).

Let me come and sing on the heights of Zion, and rejoice in the goodness of the Lord who supplies me with wheat, wine, and oil. My soil will be like a well-watered garden, and I will not sorrow anymore at all (Jer. 31:12).

Lord, satisfy my soul with abundance, and fill me with Your goodness (Jer. 31:14).

Lord, through the new covenant, put Your law in my mind, and write it upon my heart (Jer. 31:33, NIV).

Lord, search out Your sheep and take care of them. Rescue them and bring them back from the foreign nations where they now live. Be their shepherd and let them graze on fertile fields